MS Word
2007/10

Ron Greener

Computer Services

Table of Contents

Computer Services

Introduction

This book has been prepared at the request of students taking MS Word within a community education setting. It will serve anyone whose goal is to gain Word skills for the workplace, college, or just general everyday use. The author has 35 years of teaching experience at the community college level. Overlapping that to some extent are 35 years of business world experience installing and maintaining mainframe computers. The book was designed to be an exact match to the delivery of the classroom material so that repetition at a later time is 100% possible. Feedback from this concept of training has been very positive.

Notice: All Rights Reserved.

Copying the material within this book is not permitted without the expressed permission of the author, Ron Greener, greener@lcc.edu, 810-227-3839

Computer Services

Office Button

Quick Access Toolbar

8 Top Level Tabs

Ribbon of Commands

Title Bar

Close Buttons

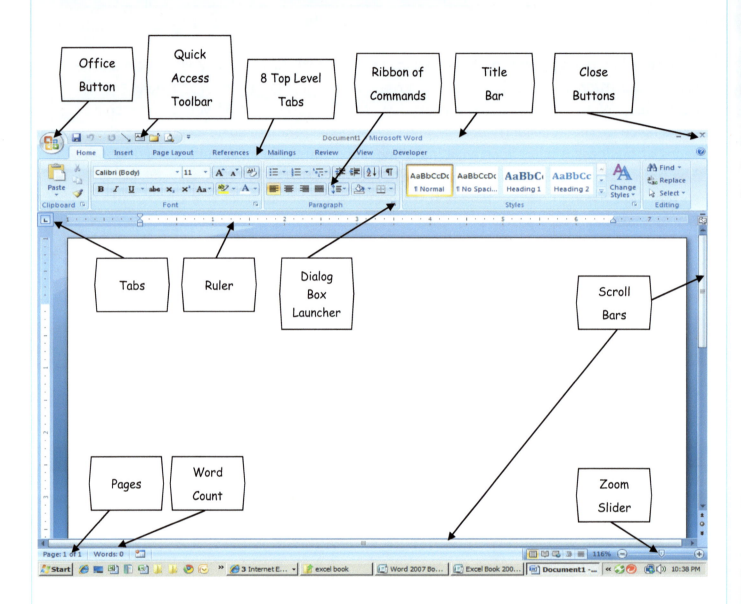

Tabs

Ruler

Dialog Box Launcher

Scroll Bars

Pages

Word Count

Zoom Slider

Computer Services

Microsoft Word 2007/10

Generating Random Text

Random Text. Frequently when you are attempting to learn a new task, sample text is required. Word has a built in command that allows for generating random text for the purpose of testing. This eliminates the need for taking the time to manually type text.

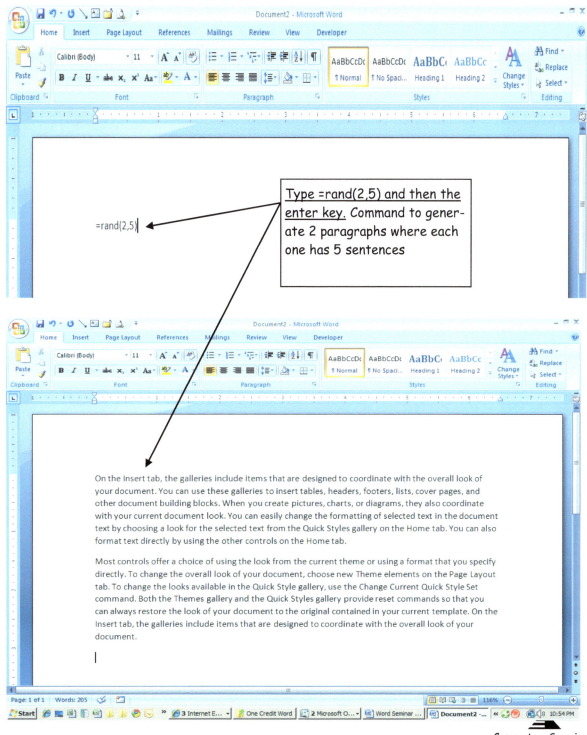

=rand(2,5)

<u>Type =rand(2,5) and then the enter key.</u> Command to generate 2 paragraphs where each one has 5 sentences

On the Insert tab, the galleries include items that are designed to coordinate with the overall look of your document. You can use these galleries to insert tables, headers, footers, lists, cover pages, and other document building blocks. When you create pictures, charts, or diagrams, they also coordinate with your current document look. You can easily change the formatting of selected text in the document text by choosing a look for the selected text from the Quick Styles gallery on the Home tab. You can also format text directly by using the other controls on the Home tab.

Most controls offer a choice of using the look from the current theme or using a format that you specify directly. To change the overall look of your document, choose new Theme elements on the Page Layout tab. To change the looks available in the Quick Style gallery, use the Change Current Quick Style Set command. Both the Themes gallery and the Quick Styles gallery provide reset commands so that you can always restore the look of your document to the original contained in your current template. On the Insert tab, the galleries include items that are designed to coordinate with the overall look of your document.

Computer Services

Microsoft Word 2007/10

Default Settings for Margins, Font, Line Spacing

This version of Word is somewhat different in how it is setup when a Word document is first opened. The character font is set to Calibri, and the font size to 11 point (11/72 of an inch vertical height). The spacing after paragraphs is set to 10 point. The line spacing is set to 1.15 spacing. The margins are all set to 1", top, bottom, left, and right. Previous versions all used Times New Roman font, 12 point, with 0 spacing after paragraphs, and margins at 1.25" left and right, 1" top and bottom.

Margins = 1"

View ruler button

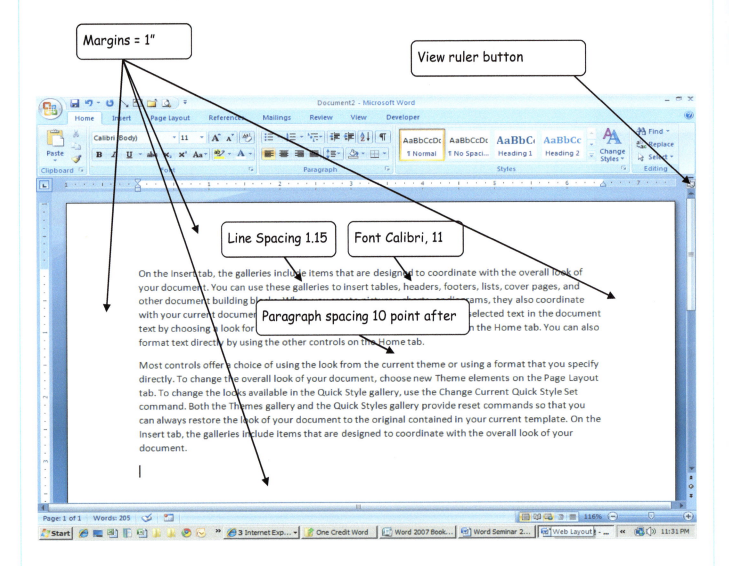

Line Spacing 1.15

Font Calibri, 11

Paragraph spacing 10 point after

Computer Services

Microsoft Word 2007/10

Setting Margins

Margins are those areas on the top, bottom, left and right sides that are reserved for white space. The exception to this is that enclosed within the top and bottom margins are header and footer areas which are meant to be used for page numbering and other such content that is to be repeated on every page of a multi-page document. In addition to making the printed page more presentable, changing the margins should be considered when attempting to squeeze more content onto a page(s) thereby creating the potential for reducing the number of printed pages.

Setting Margins

1. Click the Page Layout tab

2. Click margins

3. Select one of the presets or select Custom Margins to adjust otherwise.

4. For Custom Margins, the Page Setup dialog box allows for setting to specified values.

NOTE: GUTTER is the binding area of a book.

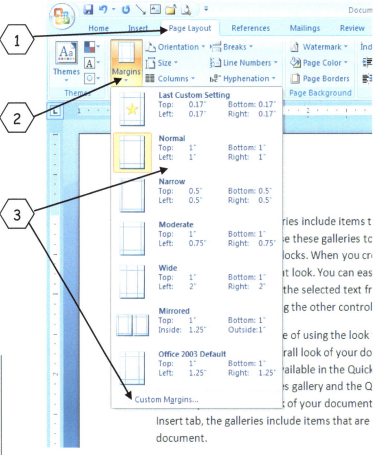

Microsoft Word 2007/10

Setting Orientation

Orientation refers to setting up the page for portrait (8 1/2 wide by 11 high) or landscape (11 wide by 8 1/2 high). Portrait is more normal but occasionally the document lends itself to being wider than it is tall.

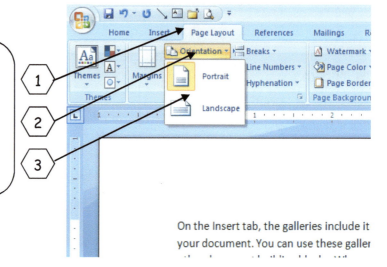

Setting Orientation

1. Click the Page Layout tab

2. Click orientation

3. Select Landscape or Portrait

Portrait

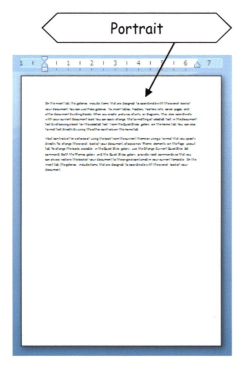

Landscape

Computer Services

Mini-Toolbar

The Mini-Toolbar appears within the document following the highlighting of text. Its purpose is to provide quick access to frequently used formatting commands. This is faster than clicking in the ribbon where selecting the correct tab and then the correct command button would take more time to do.

Mini-Toolbar

1. With the left mouse, drag thru (highlight) an area of text for which formatting is desired.

2. As you release the mouse button and move slightly, the Mini-Toolbar appears.

3. Click any one of the 14 choices

, the galleries include items that [Calibri (Bo⋯ ▾ 11 ▾ A˄ A˅ A▾ ✓ | B I ≡ ab✦ | A ▾ ⌗ ⌗ ≔ ▾] the overal headers, footers, lists, cover page blocks. Wh with your current document look. You can easily change the formatting of se text from the Quick Styles gallery on the Home tab. You can also format text

1

2, 3

Computer Services

Live Preview

In cases where formatting text involves a list to pick from, you can scroll thru the list with your mouse and Word will provide a preview of what the result would be should you select that item. This works for such commands as font, font size, font color, highlighting, and styles.

Live Preview

1. With the left mouse, drag thru (highlight) the area of text for which formatting is desired.

2. Using font as an example, open the font list. Notice that as you point to various fonts, the selected text provides a sample.

3. Try other tasks as mentioned above.

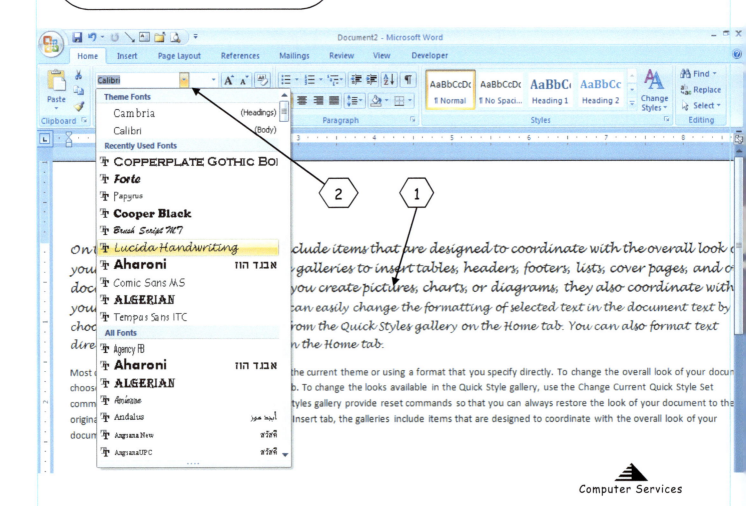

Microsoft Word 2007/10

Zoom Page

Zoom is a feature that allows for displaying more or less of the document that is being worked on. A slider in the lower right corner allows for zooming in and out. Also, by clicking on the percent indication, a window opens that provides preset zoom values such as whole page

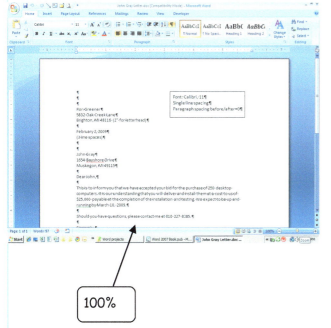

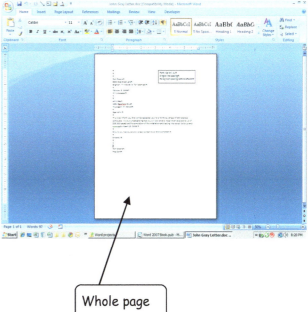

100%

Whole page

Computer Services

Microsoft Word 2007/10

Selecting (highlighting) Text

Selecting text is the process of causing it to be highlighted. It is the first step in formatting text. Whatever is highlighted is then changed when formatting commands such as font, font size, font color, bold, italicize, underline, centering, etc. are clicked. Dragging thru text with the left mouse is the most basic way of high-lighting. This page describes ways which are faster and more accurate.

On the Insert tab, the galleries include items that are designed to coordinat your document. You can use these galleries to insert tables, headers, footer other document building blocks. When you create pictures, charts, or diagr with your current document look. You can easily change the formatting of s

Select a **word** by double clicking on it.

> On the Insert tab, the galleries include items that are designed to coordinate with the overall look of your document. You can use these galleries to insert tables, headers, footers, lists, cover pages, and other document building blocks. When you create pictures, charts, or diagrams, they also coordinate with your current document look. You can easily change the formatting of selected text in the document text by choosing a look for the selected text from the Quick Styles gallery on the Home tab. You can also format text directly by using the other controls on the Home tab. ¶
>
> Most controls offer a choice of using the look from the current theme or using a format that you specify directly. To change the overall look of your document, choose new Theme elements on the Page Layout

Select a **paragraph** by triple clicking on it.

> On the Insert tab, the galleries include items that are designed to coordinate with the overall look of your document. You can use these galleries to insert tables, headers, footers, lists, cover pages, and other document building blocks. When you create pictures, charts, or diagrams, they also coordinate with your current document look. You can easily change the formatting of selected text in the document text by choosing a look for the selected text from the Quick Styles gallery on the Home tab. You can also format text directly by using the other controls on the Home tab. ¶

Select a **sentence** by holding down the CTRL key and clicking in the sentence.

> On the Insert tab, the galleries include items that are designed to coordinate with the overall look of your document. You can use these galleries to insert tables, headers, footers, lists, cover pages, and other document building blocks. When you create pictures, charts, or diagrams, they also coordinate with your current document look. You can easily change the formatting of selected text in the document text by choosing a look for the selected text from the Quick Styles gallery on the Home tab. You can also format text directly by using the other controls on the Home tab. ¶
>
> Most controls offer a choice of using the look from the current theme or using a format that you specify directly. To change the overall look of your document, choose new Theme elements on the Page Layout tab. To change the looks available in the Quick Style gallery, use the Change Current Quick Style Set command. Both the Themes gallery and the Quick Styles gallery provide reset commands so that you can always restore the look of your document to the original contained in your current template. On the insert tab, the galleries include items that are designed to coordinate with the overall look of your document. ¶
>
> ¶

Select an **entire document** by holding down the **CTRL** key and then tap the **A** key on the keyboard.

> On the Insert tab, the galleries include items that are designed to coordinate with the overall look of your document. You can use these galleries to insert tables, headers, footers, lists, cover pages, and other document building blocks. When you create pictures, charts, or diagrams, they also coordinate with your current document look. You can easily change the formatting of selected text in the document text by choosing a look for the selected text from the Quick Styles gallery on the Home tab. You can also format text directly by using the other controls on the Home tab. ¶

Select **lines** by clicking in the left margin.

> Most controls offer a choice of using the look from the current theme or using a format that you specify directly. To change the overall look of your document, choose new Theme elements on the Page Layout tab. To change the looks available in the Quick Style gallery, use the Change Current Quick Style Set command. Both the Themes gallery and the Quick Styles gallery provide reset commands so that you can always restore the look of your document to the original contained in your current template. On the insert tab, the galleries include items that are designed to coordinate with the overall look of your document. ¶

De-select by clicking in the right margin white space.

NOTEs: (1) Use the CTRL key to select non-adjacent areas.
      (2) Use the SHIFT key to select from the cursor to the point of a mouse click.

Microsoft Word 2007/10

Formatting Selected Text

On the previous page, many methods of selecting text were shown. Selected text can then be formatted. Most of the formatting commands appear in the ribbon of the Home tab. Shown below are samples of text that has been first selected and then a format applied.

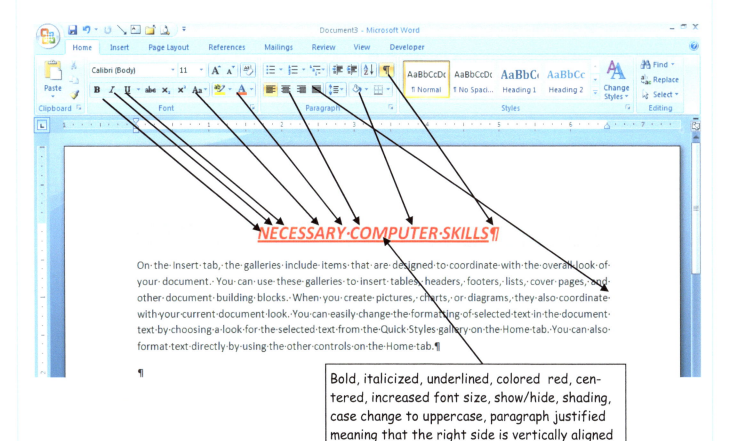

NECESSARY COMPUTER SKILLS¶

Bold, italicized, underlined, colored red, centered, increased font size, show/hide, shading, case change to uppercase, paragraph justified meaning that the right side is vertically aligned as in many books.

Computer Services

Microsoft Word 2007/10

Line and Paragraph Spacing

This feature allows for changing the distance (white space) between lines, ie single, double, triple, It also provides for adding or removing white space before or after a paragraph

Line and Paragraph Spacing

1. Highlight the desired text
2. Click the Home tab
3. Click the dropdown for Line and Paragraph Spacing
4. Select the desired line spacing
5. Select the desired paragraph spacing

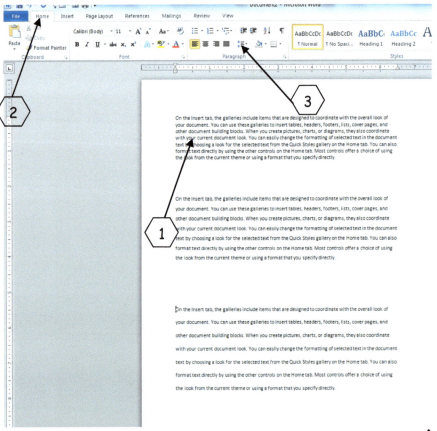

Computer Services

Block Style Business Letter

2" for header

Ron Greener
5832 Oak Creek Lane
Brighton, MI 48116 (2" for letterhead)

February 2, 2009
(2 line spaces)

John Gray
1654 Bayshore Drive
Muskegon, MI 49115

- Block style business letter, all components begin flush with the left margin.
- Font: Calibri, 11
- Single line spacing
- Paragraph spacing before/after=0

Dear John,

This is to inform you that we have accepted your bid for the purchase of 250 desktop computers. It is our understanding that you will deliver and install them at a cost to us of $25,000 payable at the completion of the installation and testing. We expect to be up and running by March 10, 2009.

Should you have questions, please contact me at 810-227-8385.

Sincerely,
(3 line spaces)

Ron Greener
President

NOTE: For the Modified Block Style Business Letter, the date, complementary close, and signature lines are tabbed over to 1/2" to the right of center.

Computer Services

Saving a Word File

Saving a document is the process of transferring a copy of the Word document which has been created in the computer's memory as a file, to the hard disk which is a permanent storage area. This is done so that when the computer is powered off, the document is not lost since it has been recorded magnetically on the hard disk. The Save As command is required for the first save so that a file name and a folder location can be specified. Saving thereafter is done by just the Save command. Note that saving should be done frequently while working on a document so that in the case of a power failure or computer lock-up, your work will not be lost.

Saving Your File

1. Click the Office button
2. Point to Save As
3. Click on Word Document
4. Type in a file name
5. Click Documents (or My Documents)
6. Click New Folder
7. Enter a name in the folder window.
8. Tap the Enter key on the keyboard
9. Click Save

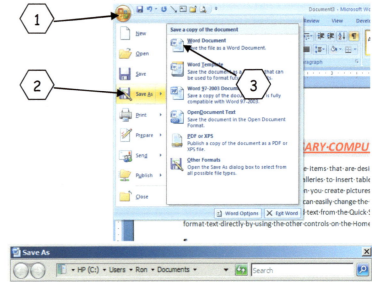

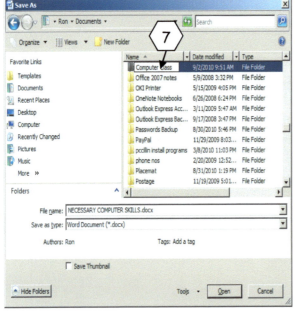

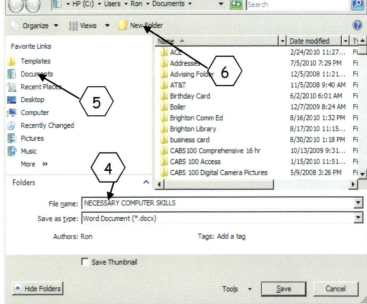

Computer Services

Opening a Saved File

A document that has been saved to the Hard Disk, can at a later time, be opened for purposes of editing, printing, saving to a different location, or giving it a new name. Opening means to transfer a copy of it from the Hard Disk to computer memory. The important fact to understand is that all files on a computer, Word or otherwise, when double clicked will open and present themselves in the application (program) in which they were created. So double clicking a Word file icon, first of all causes the Word program to open and then the Word file to open in the Word program.

Opening a File

1. Click the Start button (lower left corner of Desktop)
2. Click Documents (or My Documents Windows XP).
3. Double click the folder of interest
4. Double click the file of interest
5. Note the file is opened in Word

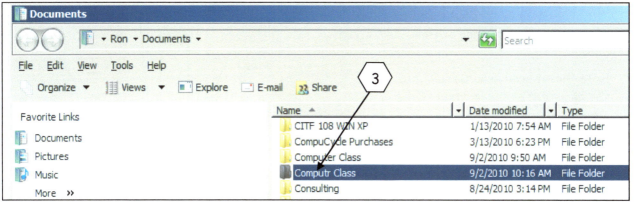

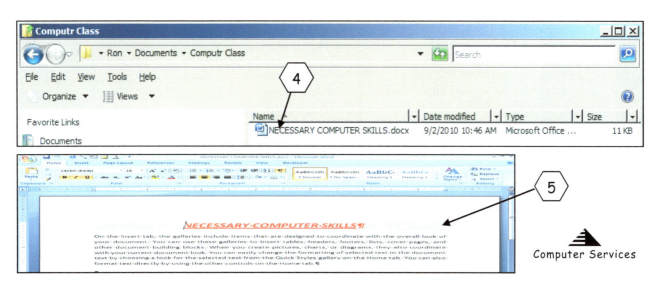

Computer Services

Inserting Clipart

Word comes with graphical images called clipart that can be inserted into a document so as to make it more interesting and appealing. You ask for clipart by entering a keyword into a search box. Word returns a list that has been retrieved from both the hard disk of your computer and from a Microsoft website. Finding one that is appropriate and then clicking on it, causes the image to be inserted into the document at the location where the cursor is located. Sizing handles (dots) appear on the borders which are used to change the size of the image.

Inserting Clipart

1. With the mouse, click the cursor at the desired location in the document.

2. Click the Insert tab.

3. Click Clipart in the "illustrations" group

4. Type a keyword into the search for box

5. Click GO

6. Click on the clipart image of your choice.

7. Note that it has been inserted into the document at the location of the cursor.

8. Alternately click the image and then white space and notice that it becomes selected and de-selected.

9. Notice that when the clipart is selected, a contextual tab appears that causes special graphical commands to appear on the ribbon.

10. Click the Home tab and then the center command button to center the clipart.

11. Place the mouse on any one of the 8 white dots and drag in/out to resize the graphic

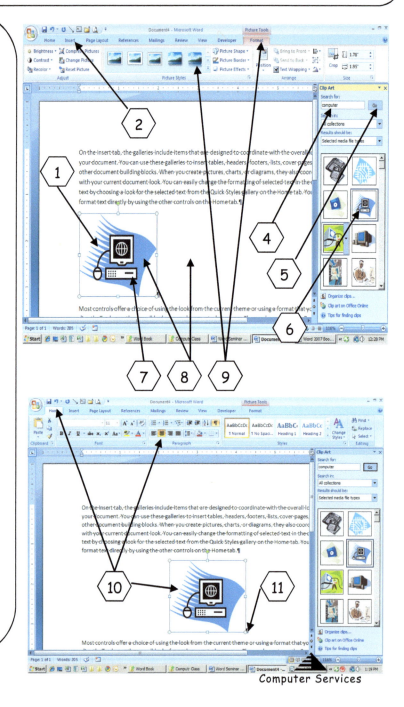

Computer Services

Format Painter

Format Painter. This feature is used to capture formatting that has been applied to certain text and then apply that formatting into other locations of the document. This is a big time saver. It also insures accuracy in making certain that the various areas have exactly the same formatting.

Format Painter

1. Select the formatted text.

2. Double click the Format Painter command. This captures the formatting in the selected text. As you move the mouse into the text of the document, notice the paintbrush attached.

3. Drag the paintbrush over the text to be formatted. Note that both are now formatted equal.

4. Click the format painter command to remove format painting from the mouse.

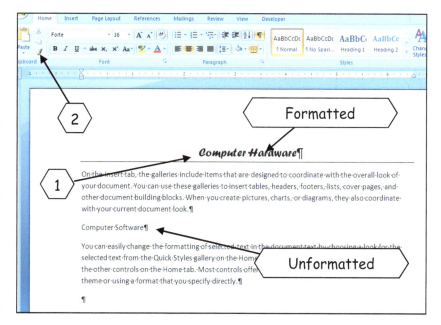

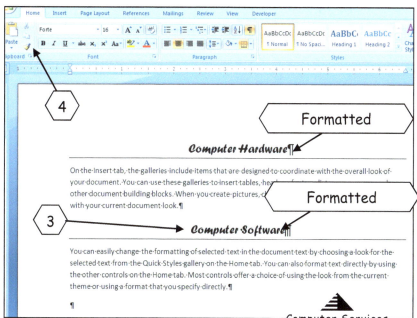

Microsoft Word 2007/10

Undo and Redo

The Undo command allows you to retract commands that have been done. This is used when the task does not accomplish the intended result. More often than not, this is a better choice that trying to fix the wrongdoing. Redo on the other hand lets you change your mind about the undoing and go back to the point where you began undoing (undoes the undoing). You can undo everything back to the start of the document. However, once you close out and then open again, the ability to undo from that point is gone. Only future tasks can then be undone.

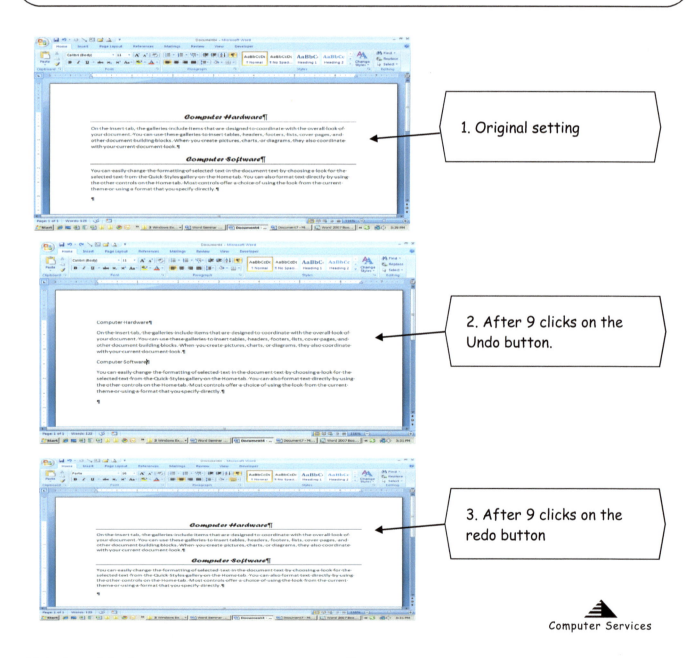

1. Original setting

2. After 9 clicks on the Undo button.

3. After 9 clicks on the redo button

Computer Services

Spell Checker. Word puts a red wavy underline under each word that it cannot find a match for in its spelling dictionary. Most of the time this means a spelling error. However, in the case of a proper name, you have to judge for yourself as to the correct spelling. Right-clicking those designated as spelling errors, provides a list of possible correct spellings that can be clicked to replace the designated word. Proofreading is especially important since some words may be spelled correctly but are out of context such as *hear* instead of *here* or *wit* instead of *with*, good spellings that would not be flagged as errors.

Right clicking Sence produces a list of possible good spellings to pick from

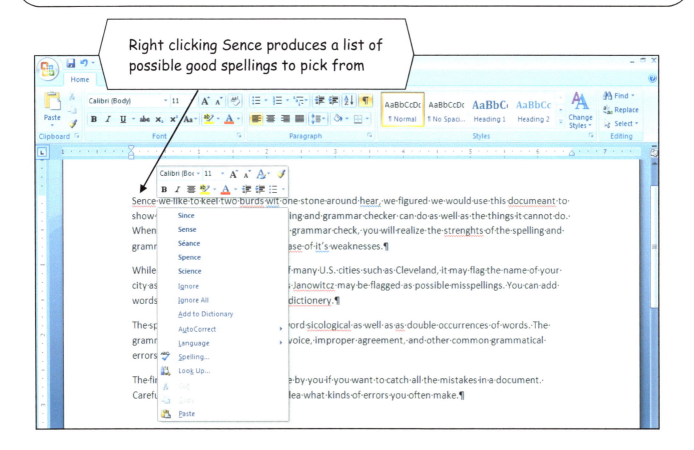

Computer Services

The purpose of setting tabs in a document is to create equal vertical alignment at the beginning of lines of text. Word has several choices to pick from: built-in tabs, left tab, right tab, center tab, and decimal tab. Setting tabs is done in conjunction with the ruler. The tab key on the keyboard is used to move the cursor to the position of the tab. When a tab is set on a particular line, then it will appear on all lines thereafter until the tab is removed.

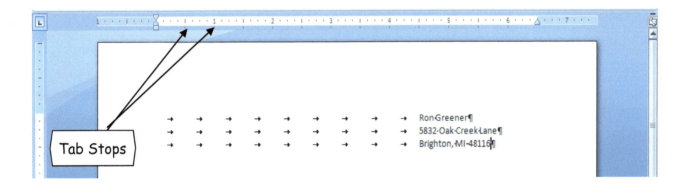

Built-in tabs. In this case the tab key was pressed 9 times to position the cursor at the 4 1/2 inch mark on the ruler. Note the bottom edge of the ruler shows small vertical marks every 1/2 inch that represent the tab stops. The 9 right-pointing arrows are an indication of tapping the tab key. They are non-printable characters that appear due to the Show/Hide being enabled.

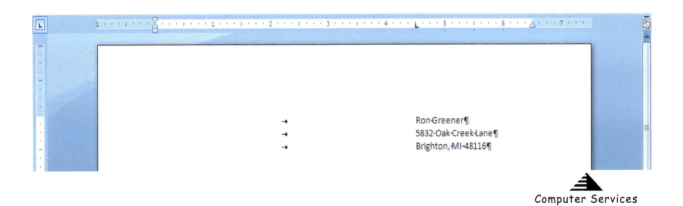

Computer Services

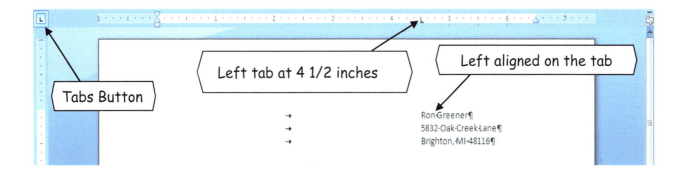

Tabs Button

Left tab at 4 1/2 inches

Left aligned on the tab

Ron Greener¶
5832 Oak Creek Lane¶
Brighton, MI 48116¶

Left Tab. In the above, the tab key was pressed only once to cause the cursor to land at the 4 1/2 inch mark. The left tab (L) was placed on the ruler by first clicking the tabs button until the left tab appears and then click on the lower edge of the ruler to place an "L" there. Note that all of the built-in tabs are now removed up to that point. After typing and when the enter key is hit to advance to the next line, the same left tab format carries down. This continues until you remove the "L" from the ruler by dragging it down just slightly. In the same manner, a center tab or a right tab can be placed on the ruler as shown below.

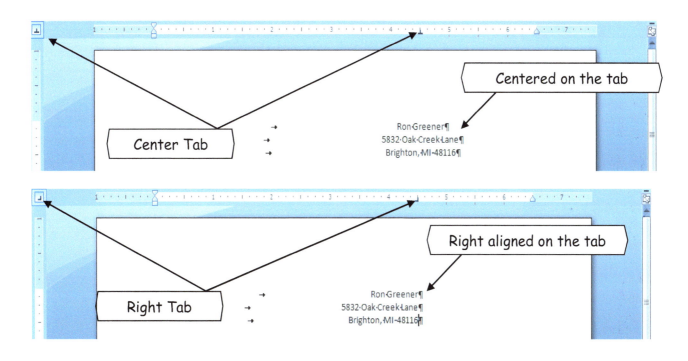

Centered on the tab

Center Tab

Ron Greener¶
5832 Oak Creek Lane¶
Brighton, MI 48116¶

Right aligned on the tab

Right Tab

Ron Greener¶
5832 Oak Creek Lane¶
Brighton, MI 48116¶

Computer Services

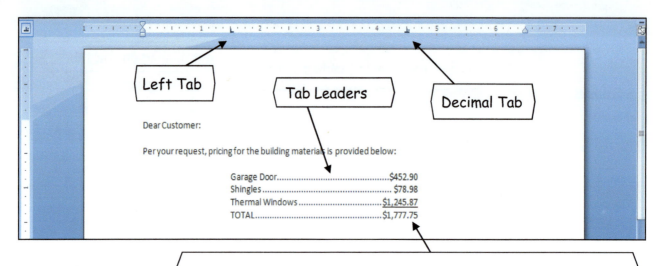

Left Tab

Tab Leaders

Decimal Tab

Dear Customer:

Per your request, pricing for the building materials is provided below:

Garage Door..$452.90
Shingles $78.98
Thermal Windows $1,245.87
TOTAL...$1,777.75

The decimal tab provides vertical alignment on the decimal points within numbers such as prices.

Applying a Tab Leader

1. Select the lines where decimal tabs appear.

2. Click on the Paragraph Dialog Box Launcher.

3. Click the tabs button.

4. Click the appropriate tab stop and the desired leader style.

5. Click ok.

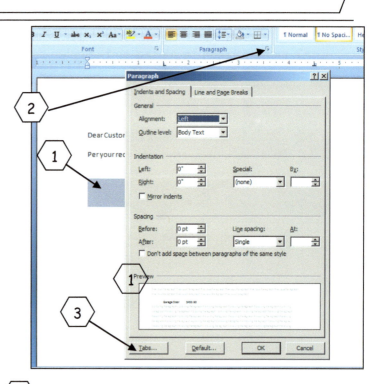

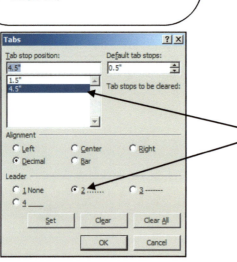

Computer Services

Microsoft Word 2007/10

Headers, Footers & Page Numbering

Headers and Footers provide the ability to enter text that will appear on every page of a document. The header is an area that occupies 1/2 inch of the top margin. Text such as page number or any text that is required to appear at the top of every page, is entered into the header and will then appear there on every page of the document. Likewise, text placed in the footer will also appear on every page. The example below demonstrates entering a name and page number in the header like that required in a research paper.

Page Numbers

1. Click the Insert tab.

2. Click Header or Footer.

3. Click Edit Header (or one of the prepared choices)

4. Right align the cursor

5. Type in your name and a space.

6. Click Page Number

7. Point to Current Position.

8. Click Plain Number

9. Verify that your name and page number are on every page of the document.

10. Click the Design tab.

11. Click the Close Header and Footer.

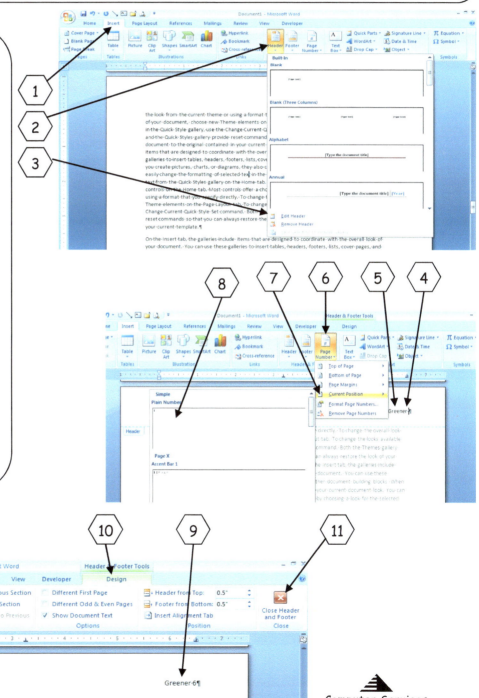

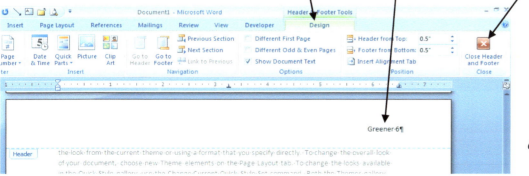

Computer Services

Borders & Shading

Borders & Shading can be applied to text such as headers to provide increased awareness of the beginning of a particular topic as shown in the example below.

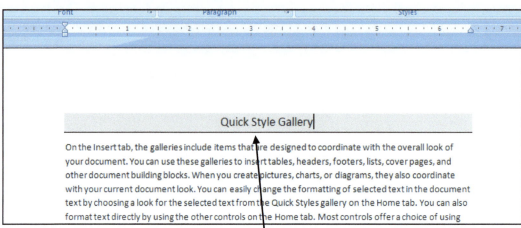

1. Enter the text in this case the title.

2. Highlight by dragging thru making sure to include the paragraph mark.

3. Center the text.

4. Apply formatting of choice such as font & font size.

5. Click the borders button.

6. Click "Bottom Border".

7. Click the shading button.

8. Click on a color of choice.

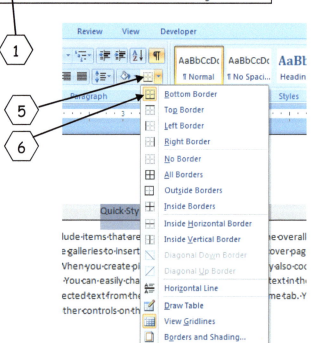

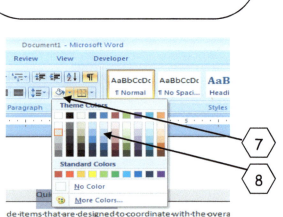

Computer Services

26

Page Borders are used to dress up announcements as shown in the announcement below

1. While in the Home tab, click on the Borders button.

2. Click Borders and Shading.

3. Click the Page Border tab.

4. Click on the Art drop-down.

5. Click on the item of choice.

6. Click on the color drop-down & choose.

7. Change the width preferred size.

8. Click Ok

9. Note that a Page Border appears around the perimeter.

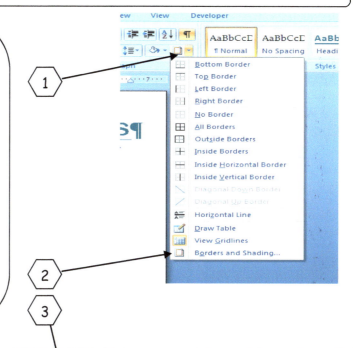

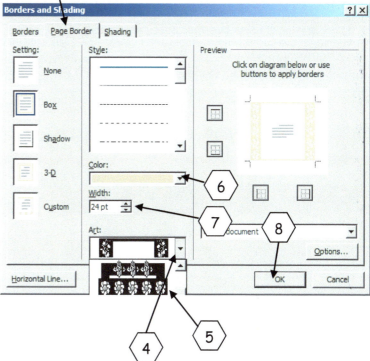

Computer Services

AutoText

AutoText is a feature within Word that allows for saving text that is frequently repeated. The example used here is the heading of a business document which typically has company information in it, ie, name of the company, logo, address info, etc. By making it an AutoText entry, it can be inserted into a document by tapping a specified key on the keyboard followed by the F3 function key in the top row of the keyboard.

Creating an AutoText Entry

1. Select the text of interest
2. Click the Insert tab.
3. Click Quick Parts.
4. Click save Selection to Quick Parts Gallery
5. Change the Gallery from Quick Parts to AutoText.
6. Enter an easy to remember character ("h" in this case)
7. Click Ok.
8. Test by opening a new sheet of paper, pres the chosen key, and tap the F3 function key located at the top of the keyboard.
9. The chosen text should appear.
10. This is now a permanent entry that can be made to appear on a document every time the chosen key is entered followed by tapping the F3 key.

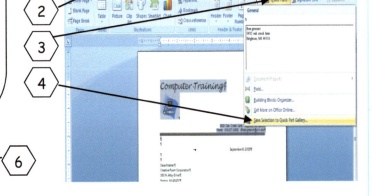

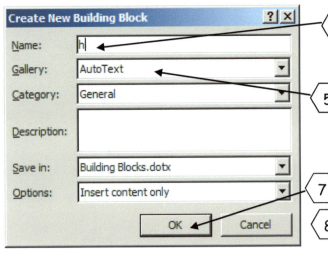

Correcting the errors in the left document below:

1. Click on the green race car & tap the DELETE key on the keyboard.

2. Highlight the top title & center it.

3. With the top title highlighted, click the Format Painter and drag thru the second title "THE HARDWARE".

4. Place the cursor after "system" in the first paragraph. Tap ENTER to create a blank line.

5. Place the cursor after "scanner" in the 2nd paragraph. Tap DELETE 4 times to remove the 4 paragraph marks.

6. Place the cursor after "microcomputers" at the end of the 2nd paragraph. Add the missing text. Tap ENTER.

7. Right-click the "appliation" misspelling. Click the correct spelling.

8. Place the cursor after "programs". Tap DELETE 3 times to remove the paragraph marks.

9. Insert a "computer" clipart in the blank line above "HARDWARE". From the Home tab, click CENTER.

10. Insert the word "basically" in the 5th line "Today there are basically..."

11. Remove the extra paragraph mark after the word "drafting" in last paragraph.

12. Check the word count for being 254.

AN·INTRODUCTION·TO·A·COMPUTER·SYSTEM¶
¶
A·computer·system·consists·of·hardware·and·software.··This·report·is·a·short·introduction·
to·the·hardware·and·software·of·a·typical·computer·system¶
THE·HARDWARE¶
¶
The·major·form·of·input·for·a·microcomputer·is·the·keyboard.··It·is·created·essentially·
like·a·typewriter·keyboard·but·it·has·many·extra·keys·such·as·function·keys·and·cursor·
movement·keys.··Other·input·devices·include·a·mouse,·floppy·disk,·and·a·scanner.·¶
¶
¶
¶
The·major·output·device·is·the·monitor·that·is·most·commonly·either·EGA·or·VGA.··
Printers·are·the·other·form·of·output.··There·are·commonly·three·kinds·in·use·with·
microcomputers,¶

THE·SOFTWARE¶
¶
The·hardware·of·a·microcomputer·is·necessary,·but·is·essentially·a·big·paperweight·
without·the·software,·or·programs,·to·go·with·it.··The·major·piece·of·software·on·your·
computer·is·the·Windows·98·operating·system·that·could·be·better·called·the·master·
control·program.·In·addition·to·Windows,·there·is·also·software·called·appliation·
programs.¶
¶
¶
Today·there·are·four·types·of·application·programs·that·are·important·for·most·
businesses;·word·processing,·spreadsheets,·database·managers,·and·graphics.··A·word·
processor·is·a·program·that·allows·the·user·to·write·letters·and·reports.··The·spreadsheet·is·
used·for·making·calculations·with·numbers·such·as·doing·your·checkbook.·The·database·
manager·is·used·for·keeping·records·such·as·an·address·list·that·is·used·for·mailing.··
Graphics·programs·are·used·for·drawing·such·as·an·engineer·might·use·for·drafting.¶

AN·INTRODUCTION·TO·A·COMPUTER·SYSTEM¶
¶
A·computer·system·consists·of·hardware·and·software.··This·report·is·a·short·introduction·
to·the·hardware·and·software·of·a·typical·computer·system¶

THE·HARDWARE¶
¶
The·major·form·of·input·for·a·microcomputer·is·the·keyboard.··It·is·created·essentially·
like·a·typewriter·keyboard·but·it·has·many·extra·keys·such·as·function·keys·and·cursor·
movement·keys.··Other·input·devices·include·a·mouse,·floppy·disk,·and·a·scanner.··The·
major·output·device·is·the·monitor·that·is·most·commonly·either·EGA·or·VGA.··Printers·
are·the·other·form·of·output.··There·are·commonly·three·kinds·in·use·with·
microcomputers,·ink·jet,·laser,·and·dot·matrix.·¶
¶

THE·SOFTWARE¶
¶
The·hardware·of·a·microcomputer·is·necessary,·but·is·essentially·a·big·paperweight·
without·the·software,·or·programs,·to·go·with·it.··The·major·piece·of·software·on·your·
computer·is·the·Windows·98·operating·system·that·could·be·better·called·the·master·
control·program.·In·addition·to·Windows,·there·is·also·software·called·application·
programs.·Today·there·are·basically·four·types·of·application·programs·that·are·important·
for·most·businesses;·word·processing,·spreadsheets,·database·managers,·and·graphics.··A·
word·processor·is·a·program·that·allows·the·user·to·write·letters·and·reports.··The·
spreadsheet·is·used·for·making·calculations·with·numbers·such·as·doing·your·checkbook.··
The·database·manager·is·used·for·keeping·records·such·as·an·address·list·that·is·used·for·
mailing.··Graphics·programs·are·used·for·drawing·such·as·an·engineer·might·use·for·
drafting.¶
¶

Plain Vanilla First Then Format

Plain Vanilla first then format. This exercise demonstrates creating a document by first entering all of the text in the default font. There should be no concern for any formatting such as font, font size, line spacing, tabs, etc. The author refers to this as "Plain Vanilla". Following that, insert graphics and apply formatting as needed.

1. Click the "No Spacing" style in the Home tab ribbon to provide single line spacing & paragraph spacing 0.
2. Type the entire document as shown on the left below, in the default font (Calibri, 11).
3. Select "Computer Training" and set the font to Lucida Handwriting, size 24.
4. Click into the beginning of the 2nd line, "Ron Greener". Tap the enter key to create a blank line.
5. Click into the blank line. Insert a clipart graphic, in this case a computer. Drag the corner sizing handle for 1" sides.
6. Select the next 3 lines and apply formatting: italics, right align, Arial, size 10 font.
7. Select just the "Phone" line including the paragraph mark. Apply a fancy border (see pg. 25, bottom choice)
8. Click prior to the date. Tap Enter twice to provide 2 blank lines.
9. Place a Left tab at the 4" mark on the ruler. Press the tab key to move the date over.
10. Click prior to "Dave Kramer" and tap Enter twice to create 2 blank lines
11. Click prior to "Dear Dave" and tap the Enter key once to create a blank line.
12. Click prior to "This.." and press Enter to create a blank line.
13. Create blank lines prior to "I can..." and before "Sincerely", and 2 before "Ron Greener"
14. Click prior to the "Sincerely" line. Place a left tab at 4" on the ruler. Tap tab on the keyboard.
15. Repeat the previous step for the "Ron Greener" line.
16. Check the document to verify that it looks like the sample on the right.

Computer Training
Ron Greener
5832 Oak Creek Lane, Brighton, MI 48116
Phone: 810.227.3839, Email:greener@lcc.edu
September 6, 2009
Dave Kramer
Creative Foam Corporation
300 N. Alloy Drive
Fenton, MI 48430
Dear Dave:
This is to inform you that I will be at your facility on October 17, 2009 to conduct a 6 hour training session on Microsoft Office 2007. I am preparing myself for a 10 student class. As per our previous agreement, the training will begin at 9:00 AM and finish at 4:30 PM, taking a 1 hour lunch from noon to 1 PM.
I can be reached at the above phone number or through my e-mail as indicated above.
Sincerely,
Ron Greener

Computer Training¶

¶

Ron Greener¶
5832· Oak· Creek· Lane, · Brighton,· MI· 48116¶
Phone:· 810.227.3839,· Email:greener@lcc.edu¶

¶
¶

→   September·6,·2009¶

¶
¶
Dave·Kramer¶
Creative·Foam·Corporation¶
300·N.·Alloy·Drive¶
Fenton,·MI·48430¶
¶
Dear·Dave:·¶
This·is·to·inform·you·that·I·will·be·at·your·facility·on·October·17,·2009·to·conduct·a·6·hour-training·session·on·Microsoft·Office·2007.·I·am·preparing·myself·for·a·10·student·class.·As·per-our·previous·agreement,·the·training·will·begin·at·9:00·AM·and·finish·at·4:30·PM,·taking·a·1·hour-lunch·from·noon·to·1·PM.·¶
¶
I·can·be·reached·at·the·above·phone·number·or·through·my·e-mail·as·indicated·above.·¶
¶
Sincerely,¶
¶
¶
Ron·Greener¶

Cut & Paste and Copy & Paste

Cut & Paste is the process of MOVING text or files from one location to another. For example, if you are writing a letter using Microsoft Word. You have several paragraphs typed. After reviewing what you have typed, you decide that the 3rd paragraph would be better placed in front of the second paragraph. You can highlight the 3rd paragraph, right-click it, click cut, right-click in front of the 2nd paragraph, and click paste, That moves the 3rd in front of the 2nd.

Cut & Paste

1. Highlight the text to be moved.
2. Right-click on top of it.
3. Click Cut
4. Click the cursor to the destination point.
5. Right-click
6. Click Paste

Copy & Paste

1. Highlight the text to be moved.
2. Right-click on top of it.
3. Click Copy
4. Click the cursor to the destination point.
5. Right-click
6. Click Paste
7. Note that a copy of the bottom paragraph is pasted on the top.

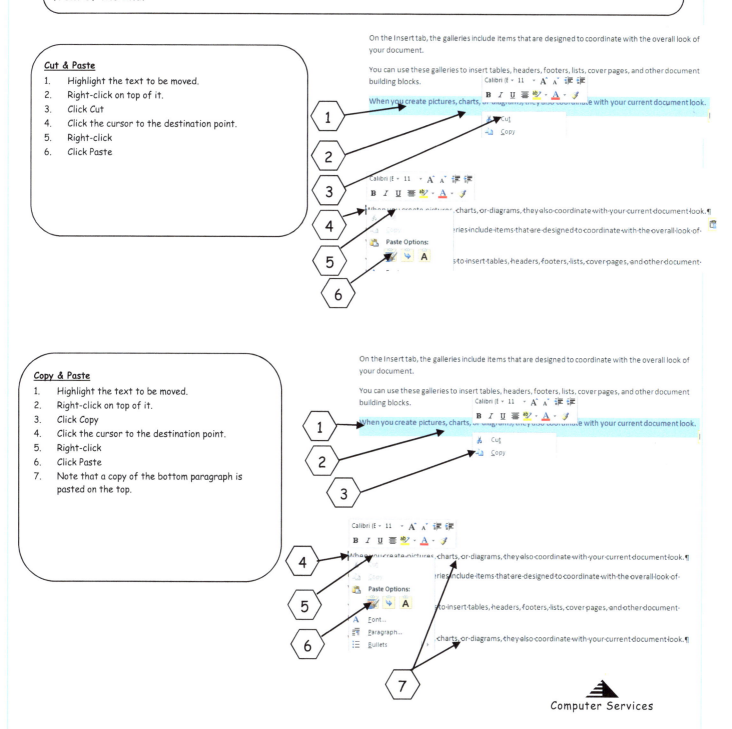

Computer Services

Microsoft Word 2007/10

Tables

A table in Word has the appearance of a piece of graph paper, ie it has rows and columns that intersect and thereby form cells (squares). The cells are used to hold data in the form of text and pictures. Rows and columns can be adjusted in width and height to accommodate the contents of a cell(s). You have the option of hiding the lines so that the use of the table is transparent when laying out data on a document. Cells can also be merged meaning that several smaller cells can be made into a larger cell.

INSERTING A TABLE

1. Insert tab,

2. Table, 6 rows, 7 columns

3. Merge the top row.

4. Enter month.

5. Center

6. Drag the bottom border to the bottom

7. Select the bottom 5 rows.

8. Distribute evenly

9. Enter the numbers for the days

10. Enter notes and graphics

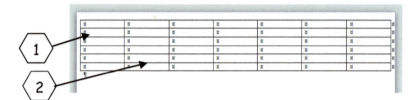

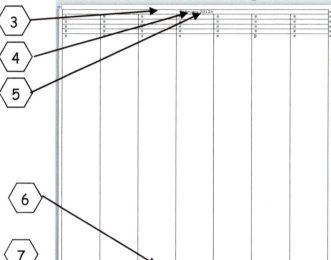

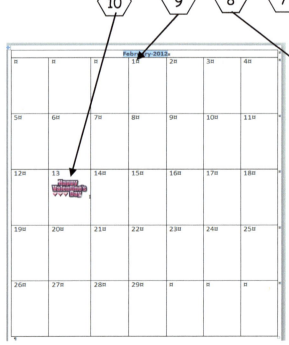

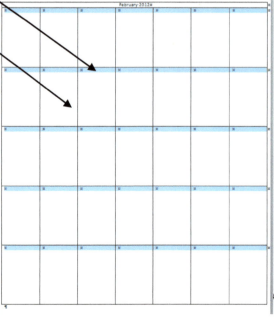

<u>**Energy Star Announcement**</u>. Refer to the next page that shows the outcome of the instructions below.

1. Enable the **show/hide** feature.
2. **Type** in the document below....allow word wrap
3. Set the left and right **margins** to 2 inches
4. Check for & correct **spelling errors (red wavy underlines)**
5. **Word count**: words _____characters _____lines_____
6. Change the **font** to **size 12, arial black** for the entire document.
7. Add **bullets** to the **two lines** under the "**LOOK FOR**"... heading
8. **Center** the two headings "**PRACTICE GREEN**"... and "**LOOK FOR**"...
9. **Change** the **font size** for the two **headings** to **14**
10. **Underline** <u>one year</u>.
11. Set the **paragraph** beginning with **The goal of** to **full justification**.
12. **Insert** a **graphic** between the **PRACTICE GREEN**... and **LOOK FOR**...headings.
13. **Center** the **graphic**.
14. Size the graphic without distorting it so that it causes the document to fully fill the page.
15. Verify that it matches the outcome as shown on the following page.

PRACTICE GREEN COMPUTING

LOOK FOR THE ENERGY STAR LABEL

25% of computer systems are left on 24 hours a day
Computers account for 5% of all commercial energy consumption

The goal of the Energy Star program is to design major computer system components that use no more than 30 watts of power when turned on but not in use. If all computers in the United States met Energy Star guidelines, enough energy could be saved to power a city of six million people for one year!

Computer Services

PRACTICE·GREEN·COMPUTING¶

LOOK·FOR·THE·ENERGY·STAR·LABEL¶

¶

- → 25%·of·computer·systems·are·left·on·24· hours·a·day¶
- → Computers·account·for·5%·of·all· commercial·energy·consumption¶

¶

The·goal·of·the·Energy·Star·program·is·to·design· major·computer·system·components·that·use·no· more·than·30·watts·of·power·when·turned·on·but· not·in·use.·If·all·computers·in·the·United·States· met·Energy·Star·guidelines,·enough·energy·could· be·saved·to·power·a·city·of·six·million·people·for· one·year!¶

¶

Buy·computer·equipment·with·the·Energy·Star· logo.¶

¶

Computer Services

Uppercase

GARAGE

Font size to 170 (as large as possible)

SALE

Center Text Horizontally & Vertically

SET LANDSCAPE, MARGINS ZERO

Page border

Computer Services

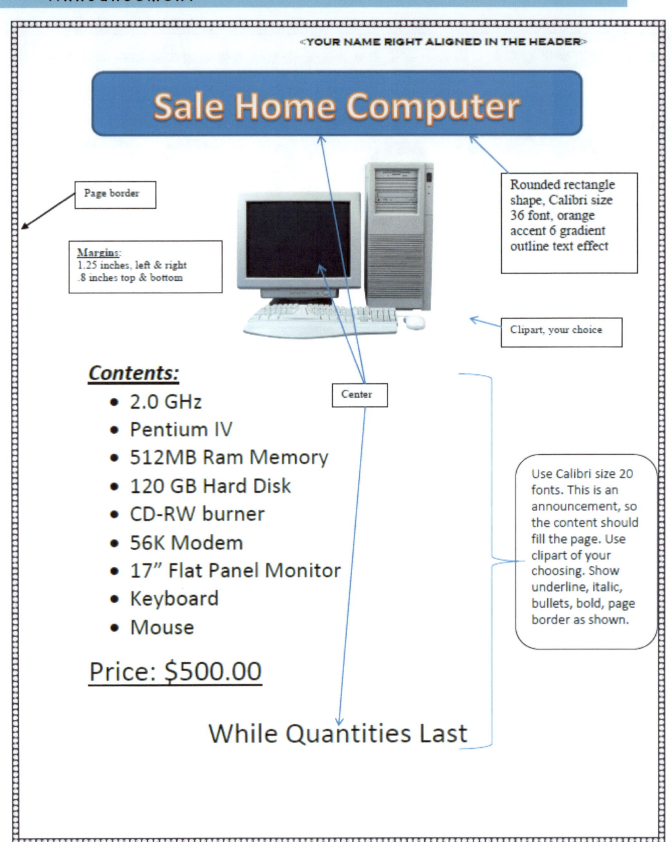

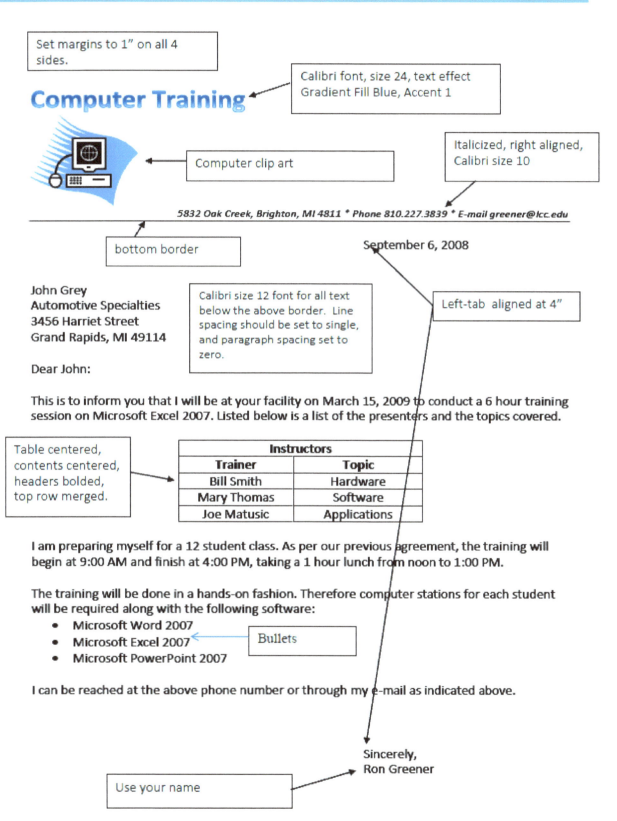

Set margins to 1" on all 4 sides.

Computer Training

Calibri font, size 24, text effect Gradient Fill Blue, Accent 1

Computer clip art

Italicized, right aligned, Calibri size 10

*5832 Oak Creek, Brighton, MI 4811 * Phone 810.227.3839 * E-mail greener@lcc.edu*

September 6, 2008

bottom border

John Grey
Automotive Specialties
3456 Harriet Street
Grand Rapids, MI 49114

Calibri size 12 font for all text below the above border. Line spacing should be set to single, and paragraph spacing set to zero.

Left-tab aligned at 4"

Dear John:

This is to inform you that I will be at your facility on March 15, 2009 to conduct a 6 hour training session on Microsoft Excel 2007. Listed below is a list of the presenters and the topics covered.

Table centered, contents centered, headers bolded, top row merged.

Instructors	
Trainer	**Topic**
Bill Smith	Hardware
Mary Thomas	Software
Joe Matusic	Applications

I am preparing myself for a 12 student class. As per our previous agreement, the training will begin at 9:00 AM and finish at 4:00 PM, taking a 1 hour lunch from noon to 1:00 PM.

The training will be done in a hands-on fashion. Therefore computer stations for each student will be required along with the following software:

- Microsoft Word 2007
- Microsoft Excel 2007
- Microsoft PowerPoint 2007

Bullets

I can be reached at the above phone number or through my e-mail as indicated above.

Sincerely,
Ron Greener

Use your name

Making Pictures Float

Typically when a picture (or clipart) is inserted into a Word document, it is said to be "in line with text". In other words it gets inserted at the location of the cursor just as if it were another character that might be typed there. You might say that it is locked there and cannot be relocated by dragging. In many cases it is desirable to be able to make the picture float so that it can be placed anywhere by dragging it around.

Making Pictures Float

1. Enter some text

2. Place the cursor anyplace.

3. Insert a picture or clipart or any type of graphic (see Insert Tab).

4. Note that the picture is locked in place, ie it cannot be dragged around.

5. Click on the picture to make it selected. It should have white dots around it (sizing handles).

6. Click on the Picture Tools Format Tab.

7. Pull down on the Wrap Text command and click Tight.

8. Hold down on the picture with your left mouse and drag. Note that the picture can be relocated and that text is wrapped around it.

9. Use a corner handle to resize it (the corner handle is used to avoid distortion).

Computer Services

Mail Merge

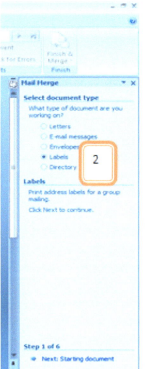

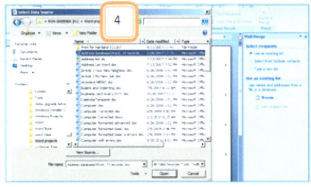

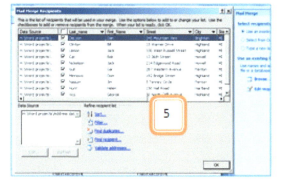

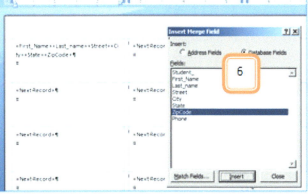

Computer Services

Paragraph Indentation

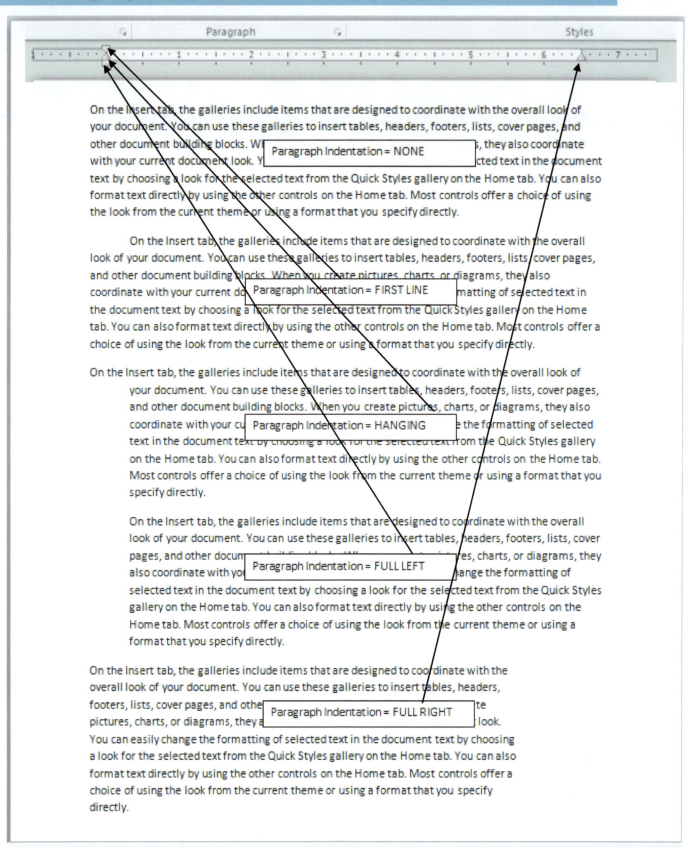

Paragraph Indentation = NONE

Paragraph Indentation = FIRST LINE

Paragraph Indentation = HANGING

Paragraph Indentation = FULL LEFT

Paragraph Indentation = FULL RIGHT